THE EMPTY LOVE LETTER

THE EMPTY LOVE LETTER

MEHAK

PARTRIDGE

ISBN: Hardcover 978-1-4828-8563-7
Softcover 978-1-4828-8562-0
eBook 978-1-4828-8561-3

Print information available on the last page.

To order additional copies of this book, contact
Partridge India
000 800 10062 62
orders.india@partridgepublishing.com

www.partridgepublishing.com/india

CONTENTS

I Hope You Enjoy Reading My Writings
As Much As I Enjoyed (& Cried)
While Writing Them. ~Mehak.

For Sophia

EXISTENCE

THE EMPTY LOVE LETTER

Scribbled notes
Poems wrote
Sleepless nights
Out of sight
Once was love
Fled away dove
Now she thinks
Her heart sinks
Days went by
Staring at sky
Months passed away
Words still slay
It's been years
Eyes get tears
Still the same
He never came
It's been long
This melancholy song
Never came the end
Letters yet unsend
Never it got better
Her life was just like-
An empty love letter.

TOO SHORT, SO LIVE

So eventually
You'll get to know
That the life we've got
Is quite too short
To mask the chores
Which are meant to be done
To mask the words
That are meant to be said
And to mask the feelings
That are meant to be heard.

BREAKIN' DOWN

You know
The worst days
Are the ones
Where sleeping away
Is the best option
And staying awake
Portrays hell.
Every single person
Contributes
To the
Breakin' down
Of Your body
Of Your cognitive functions
Of Your heart
Into a million pieces
Which can never be put back
Back the way they were..

MIRROR

I'm here
Standing right here
In front of me
I see a version of me-
Soft, gullible, naive
But that's nothing
Nothing what I actually am
I am what?
An unanswered question;
An awaited answer
Lies in here-
A TNT altogether.

CRAZY

You must be looking for a girl who
Is sweet
Has an accent
And sexy too

I am a girl with mood swings
Longing for an angel
With a broken wing

I am not the one who
sleeps with a teddy
Nor the one who
Does make-up while getting ready

I am just me
Hoping that somebody
Would also love me
Me, being Crazy

LIAR

It's actually quite funny
How we poets
Make things seem so perfect
While in reality
We may be
The most fucked up person
How we make everything look so pretty
Like, we can even make death beautiful
How we lie about our pain;
How we extract out
The bitterness
And present before you
A perfect piece of repressed sorrow
How we convert our pain; sadness
Into a miracle of words
We should be awarded
For being the ultimate liars.

FRIENDSHIP

BEST FRIEND

"Can I ask you something?" he said.
"Yeahhhhh" she answered goofily as she pulled his cheeks.
"Do..Do you love me?" he hesitated.
"OF COURSE I DO! YOU'RE MY BEST FRIEND!
I LOVE YOUUU!" she answered
and daintly squeezed his face as she brushed her lips against
his cheeks.
"Uh..No..Love as in..Love..Love.." he said and removed her hands off
his face and took hold of them tenderly.
10 seconds of silence
"I..I don't know.." she said. Puzzled.
A momentary pause
"Do you?" She asked him.
*Seconds of silence while he stares at her face, beautiful as ever;
she's smiling and blushing*
At last he says "I..I also don't know.."

Behind every "I don't know" is a gigantic mountain of secrets.
Unravelled secrets
Which demand to be heard
Heard by the person
To which your heart belongs.

But eventually these two idiots got to know
That both of them
Apparently lied
And were unaware of the fact
That they were madly in love with each other.

Best Friends?
Well, yeah-
Best at hiding feelings.

RAPUNZEL

Something in the air
Strange about this night

This night plays a mystery
A mystery yet unravelled
These lights they still haunt me
Around the world as i travel

But why is that this place-

A night deprived of beauty
A night full of scars
Like an alluring princess
Hid behind the bars

Inside her lies-
A cooled down fire
A heart full of agony
And eyes livid Sapphire

With tears of regret
She was lying on the floor
While she heard a "Knock!"
A "Knock!" on the door

In a tower so high
Who dared to come?
She got scared
And hid behind the drum

A bud of friendship thrived in-

She told him about her dreams
Of visiting the world down there
Amazed by the fact
What a beauty hid behind that fear

The festival of lights
Had just begun
The lights were mesmerizing
Like a plenty midnight suns

He glanced at her
Like there was no other
For her- he was a friend
For him- she was a forever

They both were in love
Who says miracles don't happen?
Two little love birds
Wrapped up in flushed satin..

FORGOTTEN LOVE

COBWEBS

The cobwebs woven by your love
Lay in this pit of emptiness
Dusty, untouched, black and white

Interwoven memories.

ABANDONED

I won't give up
That's what I thought
But for now onwards
I think it's time
Time for me to leave
My side of the string
As you left your side
A long time back
Which hurt
No one else but me.
Not a valid reason
I've got to love you
Not your solitary eyes
Brimming with emotions
Beckoning me to read
Read them like a book
Which I wasn't even aware exists.

Not your charming voice
That got me head over heels
I love you
And that's all I know.
You ask me how
I don't know how can I show
Because this part of me
This heart of me
Has always been yours
And will remain
Yours.
Just that I got to know it
Today-That I'm in love with you.
Truly.
Madly.
Deeply.

MASKED

What it is with me?
Why is it with me?
Becoming disconsolate lately
Why can't I just be me?

Insecure?
Maybe, but what's the cure?
So much of pessimism
but I guess there's more

Struck by oblivion
I am suffering
Stuck as an introvert
I am suffering

"Why me?"
A question too frequently asked
Obscuring the true me
Furthermore being Masked

MYSTERY

She was young
But was afraid
Often getting hurt
After all that she made

She was like a book
With too many chapters to discover
Which perhaps no one was
Able to uncover

After all that she did
The extra miles she travelled
She was just a mystery
A Mystery to be unravelled . .

IF

I know there are
Millions of miles
Between our hearts

I know that
The thing I did
I went too far

But there's one thing
That I also know
You're my "Love"
Only If I could call you so . .

(The poem 'If' is inspired by the song 'Coming Back' By Maroon 5)

SMILE

Sitting in the class.
Smiles
Travelling in the bus.
Smiles
Listening to songs.
Smiles
Studying.
Smiles
Going to sleep.
Smiles

Well, a smile can elucidate a lot.

"I wish he had known." she wished.
She wished every time she set the curve of her smile on point.

BROKEN

You know what breaks a heart?
What crumbles it like a paper?
What makes it feel dead even when you're alive?

-The fragile feelings; once intact, now broken.
-The truth left unspoken.
-The unkept promises that weep.
-The bitter lies from the deep.

FLAMES

I could build a galaxy
With the words i left unsaid
My love for you; you tore apart
Burnt down in flames; unread.

TRUTH

Your lips
They say you love me
But your eyes
They say a lot

With the words of eyes
I interpret
The truth is
That you not.

NEVER II

"NO!!!! I DON'T LOVE YOU!!!
DID YOU GET THAT?
I NEVER DID." He Confessed.

A tear trickled down from her eye like a melancholy silver bead.
Commenced from the dark crevasse of secrets; her eyes.

"Never?" She asked.
"Never." Said He.

CRIPPLED

Gazed at me with fiery eyes
Stood there like the moon
And watched me as i get
Crippled by my cocoon.

FORBIDDEN HEART

I took a chance
To love you
I looked at you
A love so true

I took a chance
To *fall for* words
I looked at you
Those three I heard

I took a chance
Have been a *fool*
I looked at you
It pours out; it drools

I took a chance
I tried
I looked at you
I cried

I took a chance
I did
But now my heart
Has to *forbid*.

MOMENTS

CLICK

One Click away
I gathered the guts
And to my astonishment
I went all grey

Your looks
Your style
Those eyes
With that smile

It struck me hard
Right here, in my heart

It seems as if I am being deceased
Out of one's misery
I'll be pushing up daisies . .

MAGIC

A young couple,
Sitting at the edge of the stairs
Of the rooftop
Gazing at each other
In the rain
Which seems to be neverending-

"Haha you can tell me everything alright; I won't bite you!" he chuckled
and looked at her admirably.
"That's the thing.." she glitched
"What?"
"I might bite you!" she laughed
and leaned in for a kiss.
A kiss that both of them were unaware of.
A kiss which was burried under the weight of books for so long.
A kiss which was meant to be.
A kiss which collided with the stars.
A kiss which made them feel close to one another.
A kiss which embarrassed both of them, yet, never
wanting to leave another, still, holding on tight.
A kiss which embraced both of them in a loving way no one ever could.
A kiss which made them feel millions of sets
of emotions at the same moment.
A kiss is what it was.
Magic is what they felt.

TROUBLE

"What are you?! You make me go crazy!
I can't stop thinking about you!!
I just can't. Tell me, WHAT ARE YOU!???" he exclaimed.

"Trouble." she whispered.

LOVE

"What is love?" she questioned.

"It's a thing for fools."

One Year Later

"I Love You."

BOOK

"There's this book i'm reading these days. It's
the most beautiful one i've ever read.."
"Ohhhhhhh! Which one???"
"You."

SKY SHOT

The sky shot filled the black sky with pixie-dust.

"Look! It's so beautiful!" She shouted!

Beside her stood he.
Watching her face as it gets illuminated by the night light.

"I know right, so beautiful.." He smiled.

WORLD

"Why do you keep on writing about me when
you've got the whole world to write about?"

"That's precisely what i'm doing. You. You are my world."

PASSION

TONIGHT

Tonight
The golden eclipsed moon
Is descending
Into the arms of the sea
The way he smiles at her
The way he's approaching her body
The words are better left unsaid
When their eyes are saying it all
That
For how long they've longed for each other
For how long they've been waiting
For this night to arrive
This would be the night
The night of complete stillness
Where the sun would kiss the waves
Where they will make love; sacred love
And just as they wished
They would be one
May it be for a fraction of a second
May it be for a little longer
But they would be one. Together.

THIEF

Like a thief you stole my heart
And kept it in a jar
An eye of an artist; a piece of an art
You drew each crumb, each scar

SPARKLES

You're the one
Who adds
Sparkles to the stars

You're the one
Who tries
To heal my scars

Overlooking my flaws
Ignoring the foes and awes

You're the venus star
That shines so bright
You're the one who
Emits his own light

REIGNITE

You're the spark
Light the fire
Within you
Around you
Let them admire

You're the light
That shines so bright
Uphold the shine
Let the dark consign

One day dark
And one day light
Leave your mark
And Reignite

BOX

Can I just pick you up
And dump you
In a box
Pack you up
With stars and glitters
Hide you from the world
And gift all of you to myself?
Allow me to..

I WILL

I am going to decorate you
Not with stars and glitters.
I am going to sing to you
Not melodies and songs.
I am going to *fight for* you
Not with arms and weapons.
But you know what?
I am going to love you
With all *of* my words.
I will sing to please you
With the best ever poems I've had.
I will decorate every iota *of* you
Like you're the tree on a Christmas Eve
I will decorate every iota *of* you
With magical words and sparkling phrases.

MONSOON

Sweet talks
Best friends
Long walks
Hands held

Rain talked
Drenched clothes
Lips locked
Love- floats.

MERGED

The rain came down
And lit up the flowers
Two souls merged into one
Eternal love; one scar.

DROWN WITH ME

Drown with me
Into the depths
Of my eyes

Drown with me
Into the oceans
Of the skies

Drown with me
With every breath
That i take

Drown with me
With every poem
That i make

Drown with me
Into the darkness
Of the night

Drown with me
So that i could
Voice with a sigh-

You were my first
You were my last
My only future
My only past.

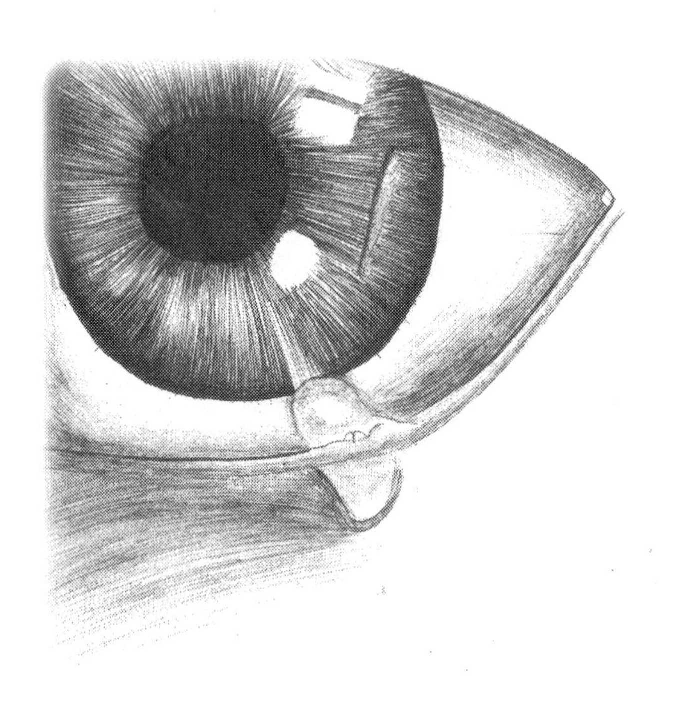

REMINISCENCE

DARK

You're perfect
Just like that

With those -
Ruffled hair
And honey lit skin
Happiness in the air
More than an angel akin

But somehow
I miss the you
That I once knew

'Cause we are we -

You are you
And I am I
Completely in love
With our Dark sides . .

WAIT

Grey clouds
Approaching the night sky
Which somehow
Remind me of your eyes.

With tears that roll down my cheeks
Blending with the rain
Tasting every iota of it
Kissing away my pain.

I'm still waiting
Standing, drenched in the rain
Longing for my love
To take away my pain

TIME

I thought-
We'd never
Fall apart

But my thoughts
Not forever they'll last

I thought-
I'd never
Be left alone

But again, my thoughts
I wish I had known

'Cause just like the time
People too change

It was time that changed me
It was time that changed us
In a perplexing way
That it still hurts.

REMINISCENCE

Look at the sky
The night sky
The sky full of depth
Just like your eyes
Just like your talks
The reminiscence still remains.
Can you smell the rain?
As fresh as it could be
Take deep breaths
Feel it
Rushing through your blood
The freshness
The tenderness
The pain
The agony

A whole set of emotions
Some known
Some unknown
Striking
At the same moment.
Can you see the lightning?
Can you hear the thunder?
These are my feelings
Pleading to get known
Known by you.
My only fantasy
Is to remain by your side
And be with you
From the beginning
Till the end.

WORLD II

The weather, my love
Is cold and dark and shivery
With my heart it could be twinning
Let your beautiful eyes
Run through the sky
It's glowing tangerine
With a tinge of sparking purple
And twinkling lights that follow
You might end up watching
A broken pearl necklace;
From which a mourning pearl
Has been left behind
The light of which alone
Illuminates the darkness
And you my darling, you
Arouse this tingling sensation
In the latent part of my chest
Which makes my senses go numb
And all that I can see is
Your face, bright as the moon
Glistening your light upon me
And illuminating my soul; my world.

NEVER

When the sky turns dark
You're all I'm ever thinking about
Wondering if you were here
Together, a new story we would embark

Recalling that time
When you were here with me
That fragrance of yours
And those eyes that Never saw me . .

DREAM

Was there a time
When just a sight of you
Made me blush and blue?

Was there a time
When just a whiff of your perfume
Made me chuff and bloom?

Was this time actually there?
Or was it a Dream floating in the air?

Now where has this time gone?
Creating a void
Leaving me forlorn

YOU

But still there's a part of me
That will always love You
A part of Me
Will remain
A part of You . .

A BEAUTIFUL SOUL

I'll admire your beauty
And fossilise it in pages
Alas we're against each other;
Against our own rages

ENVELOPED

One day
You mean the world to them
And the next
You pass each other as strangers

One day
You can't live without them
And the next
You quote each other as haters

But what about-
Those stolen glances
Those pretty chances
That somehow
Revamped into ashes

A feeling so jittery
A feeling so bitterly
Which perhaps
Enveloped the fire in me . .

BEAUTIFUL

You were like a dream
Which miraculously came true

I know I could never find someone
Someone as good as you

Even in my wildest fantasies
Even in this stupendous galaxy

You're Beautiful
And you know that
Don't you?

TODAY

Day and night she wrote
With uttermost ease-
His eyes like amber
His hair like breeze

Days and nights of crying
Those eyes got sore
Days and nights of crying
They last no more

But today seemed like a new Today-

Where there's no We
Just I
There's no Love
But Life
He's no longer here
Strangers, Strangers everywhere

That today was a day
When all she did was pretend
That today was a day
Time could never mend.

EMPTY DREAMS

You owe me your love
All of it you do
As i am swinging between
These empty dreams of you.

YOU AND I

I wish my life was a poem
Because poems they never die
Just like our love
Just like you and I.

(Inspired by the song "Last Song Ever" by SecondHand Serenade)

A TALE

You told me about love
How you were never loved
And how badly you wanted
To be loved unconditionally
By someone special

You told me about love
How afraid you were
To love someone
As everybody you loved
Left you, with a deep void
Inside your heart; your soul

You told me about love
How you used to stand
Near the tree
And watch me read a book

You told me about love
How you used to
Admire my face from a distance
Like it was all that you wanted

You told me about love
How you gathered the guts
To walk up to me
And initiate a talk

You told me about love
How crazy you were going
On the inside
When we first had a conversation

You told me about love
How fast your heart raced
When i flashed a smile

You told me about love
How afraid you were to lose me

You told me about love
How difficult it was
To find words
To write about me

You told me about love
How you fixed
A picture of you and me
In your wallet

You told me about love
How beautiful i looked
With my messy hair

You told me about love
How you played with my hair
While i was deep asleep

You told me about love
How every touch of mine
Made you feel hysterical

You told me about love
How my body fragrance
The fruity fragrance
Instantly made you blush

You told me about love
How everything went blur
When i dragged you into a dark corner
And kissed away your pain

You told me about love
How paralyzed your body felt
When we both made love
In that room of yours

You told me about love
You told me about all
Don't be afraid, my darling
I'll catch you when you fall.

YOU II

You are what to me
The thorns to a rose

You are what to me
A garden with weed that grows

You are what to me
A wrecked ship on the shore

You are what to me
Satisfaction; but longing for more

You are what to me
A sundress in the field

You are what to me
An armor with its shield

You are what to me
The rays to the sun

You are what to me
The laugh to the fun

You are what to me
The blue to the sky

You are what to me
Wings of birds; they fly

You are what to me
The tears to my pain

You are what to me
The blood rushing down my veins

In words I can't explain
What to me you are
Maybe the words to my poem
Is what you really are

UNREADABLE

"Nice handwriting out there.."

"Haha! It seems pretty but it's just unreadable!"

"Just like you, right? Pretty and unreadable.."

CONCEALED

My hands are tied
My lips are sealed
Your profound secret
Lies in here concealed

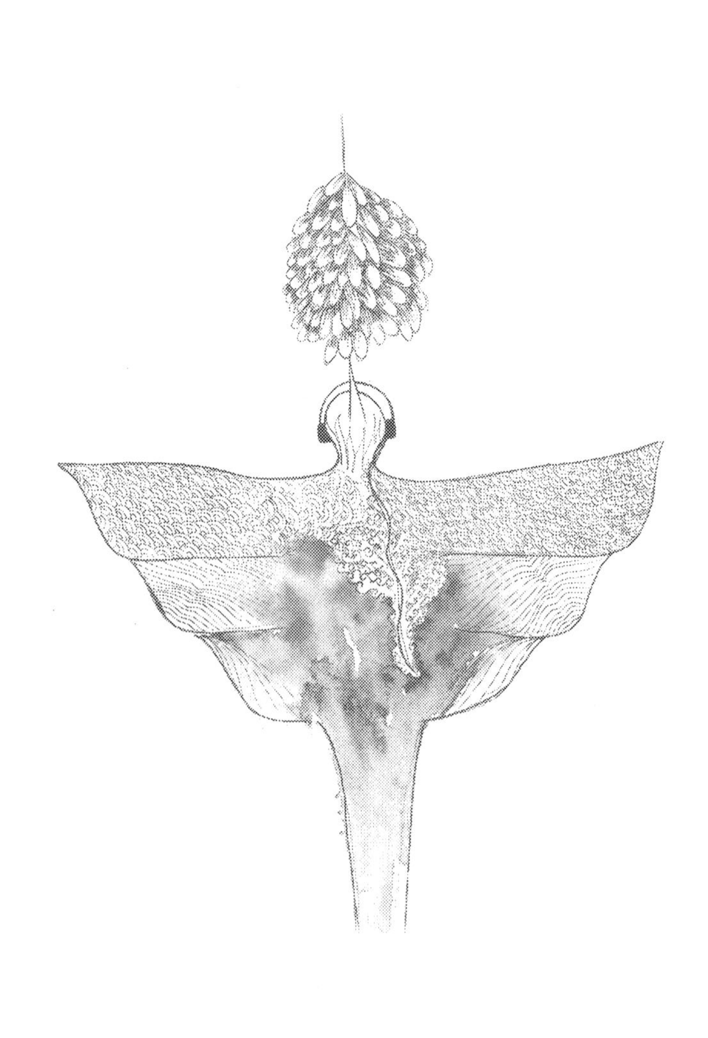

SEEKING

AMBER

Where did that love go?
Which used to descend from your eyes

Your eyes –
Brimming with your love for me

Your face -
Ochre eyes were all that I could see

Where did that promise go?
Not to see a tear in my eyes

Impossible for me to believe
That you're the reason behind these

Because . .

What else is left now?
In those eyes that somehow
Had that spark

Are now full of-
Hate? Anger?
Which once used to lighten,
Lighten like Amber . .

CHANCE

Let's take a Chance
Together we might
Give flight
To that old kite

Let's take a Chance
And along the beats
Of our hearts
Shall we dance?

Let's take a Chance
For one last time
And this time it'd be sweet
Like a rhyme

Sweet and melodious . .

ALL

Your heart knows things
Your mind can't explain

Your heart it dies
Watching me in pain

Your eyes knows tears
Hid in lock for years

Your lips can't wait
The tingling taste awaits

All you need is me
Come back; take all of me.

FREE

You're like a fish
Lost in the sea
One day you'll be caught
One day you'll set free.

NATURE

FAVOUR

All night, all alone
Thoughts that haunt me
Make me forlorn

Soon time will pass
It's a phase of life
Oh lord, please make it fast

Soon it will be all over
Good omens and blessings will hover

All around us
All in Favour

SEASONS

Every now
Will somehow
Be transformed into then

Every day
Curse yourself
Questioning- what and when?

Many will come
Many will go
Many will stay afloat

Everything that happens
Happens for a reason
Even the stunning nature
Changes its Seasons.

THE MOON

Like a solitary pearl
He hid behind the clouds
Within his mind, a hushed tranquility
Shouting out, loud

He once told me-

He was -
As dark as the sky above us
As deep as the ocean we see

Under the crimson love
Of his beloved one
He picked up the path
Of gats and guns

So many lives he took
Of unimpeachable smiles
Love for mankind he mistook
With the deleterious ruby isle

Later he gave a thought
It wasn't the thing for him
Left away with words unsaid
And tears filling up to the brim

Invigorating october breeze
Left him in a deep turmoil
Distress falling of the leaves
Made him cry for torn memoir

A momentary pause
Left him in a daze
With a silent lapse he stood
Thinking about
The words and promises
He never kept but could

From that moment on
When he went away far
From that moment on
I'm in love with his scars

RIVER

I sat on the bank
With a cold, dark shiver
While my tears filled up
The long dried river.

NIGHT GARDEN

The Night Garden
The one you see above
Is an abode of secrets
An abode of stars and love

CONSTELLATION

From my window I could see
A tiny star up there
With none others around
A solitary drop of silver
Confined within his system
Preoccupied by his mind
Oblivious of what's around
But he's one of a kind
Instead of being a part of one;
He'll build his own constellation

THE ZEPHYR

You were endowed by the ocean
A mild, cool breeze
Jillion smiles you revived
Myriad souls you pleased

You swirled through the plains
Gave flight to the birds
To a galore of poets you bestowed
Their vital weapon- words

You jaunt past the woods
Like a rapturous zing
The vines through the boulevard
A placid path they swing

Then you climbed the glorious hills
And helped the creamy clouds
To bring down the blizzard
And gratify the crowd

To hush-hush the souls
At last you went away
And recast your path
Back to the bay.

ALCHEMY OF THE SKY

Have you ever seen
How it brews with the dark
Embellished in the best attire
Connate a dazzling monarch

Did you give a thought
How he never left the moon
While the moon wept and cried
Which hence, bought the monsoon

In the glistening light of the sun
Where the stars fade and dispel
It's hard to even glance at it
It's a voodoo; it's a spell

But somehow i'm in love
With this alchemy of the sky
I wonder how it's done
I wonder how and why

SAD GOODBYES

MISSED

Are those your arms?
Take me in
Are those your lips?
Let the magic begin

You took me in your arms
Mesmerized by your charms
You own my heart,
With a new beginning
A new start

Was it my fault?
That I expected too much?
Too much it never was
Just wanted you back
Back in touch

I wanted us to be like,
What we used to be before
Wanted to a fly a kite,
That was never flown
But I am afraid to say,
That we both have grown
Sorry my darling,
But now the grenade has blown

Catch me if you can,
'Cause I'm not the one to be Missed
Now I think it's time for you to go away,
Because your part in my life has finished.

END

"You're perfect.
And you know that,
Don't you?" she asked coyly.

"No i don't, tell me, what am I?"

She remained silent.
He got his answer.
Sometimes, it's not that easy to fathom feelings into words.

A story came to an end
Before it had begun.

THE UNKNOWN WORLD

When we die
We just move
From one world
To another.
When I die
Just hoping
I'd find the one
I was looking for.
All of this world
Searching for you
Everywhere.
Maybe some day
We'll meet again
And relive the moments
Once again.
If not this world
Then some other maybe
Maybe I'll find the one
The one I was longing for.

FOREVER

I know i pushed us away
From the 'Forever Trail'
But my words-they still speak
Forever they prevail.

ONCE-LOVED-STRANGER

Remember me, will you?
As your Once-Loved-Stranger.

HAPPY ENDS

I've been laying in my bed
Wanting it to be over
The demons inside my head
Round and round they hover

There are times when the pain subsides
At times i make it hush
But still it haunt my insides
My thoughts it tends to crush

Oblivion filled the space
It's hard to hear the silent scream
The love was left in traces
The eyes forget to dream

The moon sacrificed his light
To the lilac sky
I lost my sleep; my nights
Just to give it a try

I've been crippled in fear
To see how it ends
It's so loud in here
No more the 'Happy Ends'

GOODBYE

Take me there
Where we'll taste the stars
Take me there
Where we'll watch the happy flowers

Where the sky shines bright;
A sparkling moonbeam
A place nearby
A place in my dreams

Will you take me there?
Would you leave or stay?
Left my question unanswered
Alas, you went away

It's quite saddening
How we seek for "whys"
I'm longing for that night
With no sad goodbyes.

AT DEATHS' DOOR

TILL THE LAST BREATH

Beautiful and breathtaking
There was this girl
"Pihu" was her name
Her face radiant like a pearl

Studious she was
Reading books all the time
Never questioned her parents
Will she have her time?

Romance novels were
Her favourite of all
She used to read-
Girls are treated as barbie dolls

She grew up and started studying
For medical entrances
Never even knowing
What may or may not be her chances?

She got selected
Jumped with pride and joy!
But her heart says-
She's gonna meet her dream boy . .

Her heart pounded
When she sat for the examination
Was it just her
Or anybody else
Who was feeling that sensation?

Her hands stopped working
Like they have no living
Before she could know
What's happening
She found herself
Down on the tiling

She didn't know what happened next
Neither did she wanted to know . .

Unfortunately,
This bubbly little miss
Was diagnosed with
"ALS"

It was a fatal disease they say
For her parents
It's no difference between night and day

On the bed, pale and dull

Almost dead
Deep inside her thoughts
Charming Dr. Armaan
And her eyes got caught

Risking his license
He treated her medically
She got healed
And they both
Got attached emotionally

They fell in love
In the most unexpected circumstances
Doctor-patient fell in love
Are there any chances?

The pain was extreme
That she could not bear
All that she was facing
Was not at all fair

She died.
A very painful
And unexpected death
Dr. Armaan stopped taking care
Of his health

He was all broken
He was all shocked
This was a traumatising experience
For his heart

On that day
He swore,
Swore on his death
He will love Her,
Love Her Till His Last Breath . .

This is the poem version of the book "Till The Last Breath" written by Durjoy Datta.

ALIVE

I know I'm doing it wrong
But this is where I belong

I try hard to manipulate
But just can't cope up
Feelings, emotions
Just vague notions

Can't see any open door
Can't see any light
Don't want of it anymore
Just want to end this night

No way out I could figure
No way in to survive
I have my finger on the trigger
Just don't hope of me being Alive . .

GONE II

Don't you ever wish
That you'd just sleep
And never wake up?
Don't you ever wish
To just runaway
Away from this plastic world
And just leave behind everything
Just as it is?
Don't you ever wonder
Who'd notice
When you're gone?

OVER

Threw it hard
No more it is

Red all Over
All over red

It's Over, it's Over
But we're certainly not;
Not yet Over.

DEAD

The twinkling of the stars
The falling of the leaves
The darkness of the night
The freshness of the breeze

All signify the mishappening
Going to take place-
With the pale fingers
And wrinkled face

Soon turned into
A lifeless
Bundle of
Sadness
Men-they head home
Moon-left alone
Sky-it glows red
Alas, she's dead.

SUICIDE

For her it was difficult to live
Than it was to die
During the span of all four seasons
All that she did was cry.

"Nothing to hide" she used to say
Amazingly she stood so tall
Fear engulfed her thoughts and ways
With no attempts to fall.

In the end she was dying inside
With guilt embedded within
Nothing to hide; nothing to hide.
And a smile; angel akin.

There was a way to escape
The only way was- Suicide
With the reminiscence of all the beautiful memories
A peaceful death she died.

PISTOLE

Thinking about the letters
Those i never sent to you
All of these unsaid words
Which led me to the blues

With feelings of animosity
And words i write with love
I write this poem for you
Kindred a mourning dove

A fire provoked within me
A tall stature it rose
Flourished a flame tree
Feeding it with enmity; it grows

Perpetually strikes my soul
An eternal visceral of bliss
As i took out my pistole
And sunk into the deep abyss..

SAVE

Post Midnight Talks

2:00 am

"It's Friday The 13th.." she whispered.

"Are you scared?"

2:01 am

"Hello?"

2:02 am

"Hello???!!!"

3:09 am

"Sorry Sir, We couldn't save her.." Said the doctor.

SOUL

She lies on the floor
Dipped in transient love
Her eyes wide open;
Fingers grasping the knife
Blood runs out of her
Like water from the peaks
Her eyes held the tears
Her mouth held the words
She took the path
Unchosen by many
The soul left the body
The soul, lost and puny

LAST WORDS

The last words i want to say
Is that the love we shared was true
As you loved me when i was invisible;
Loved me when i was unable to..

POEMS

ACKNOWLEDGEMENTS

An idealist teen with a tempestuous imagination.

Never in my dreams I'd imagine this happening. Quite a dreamer I am. I'd like to thank my Ma for never giving up on me whenever I used to have a breakdown and was unable to write more, Devashri for tolerating my revolutionary mood swings, Asha Aunty or shall I say, my Godmother for making my dream come true and Manish Uncle for clicking this wonderful picture of mine. And at last, how I can forget, Sandhya Subramanian for letting me use her exquisite illustrations for my first book.

Thank You All For Your Support. Without You, All Of This Would Have Been Impossible.